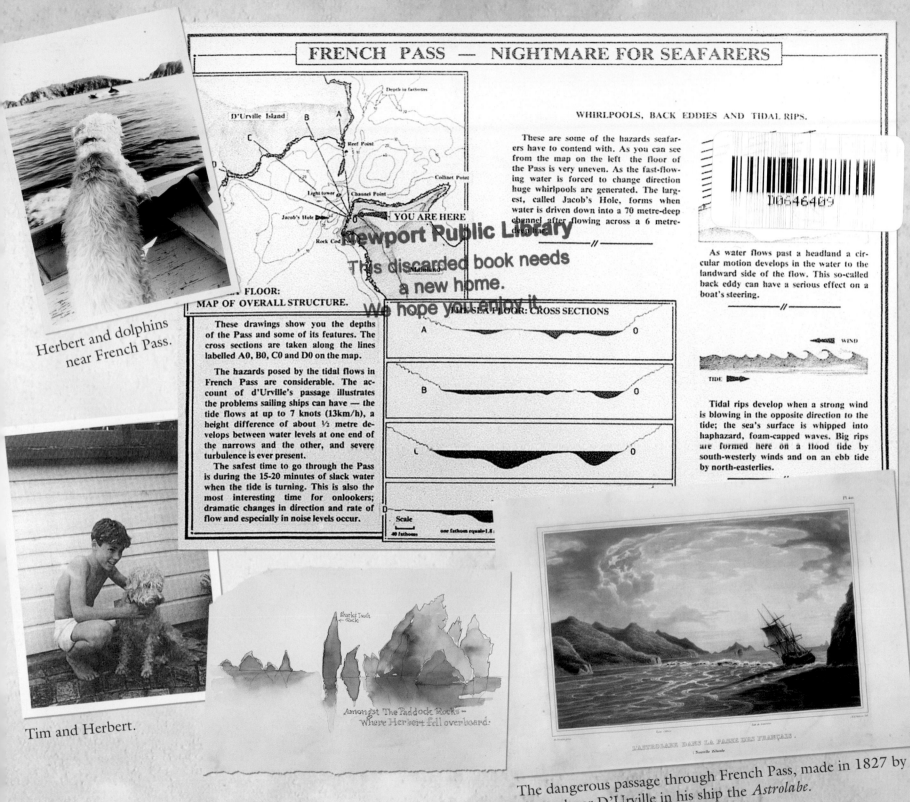

FRENCH PASS — NIGHTMARE FOR SEAFARERS

D'Urville Island

Reef Point

Collinet Point

Light tower Channel Point

Jacob's Hole

Rock Cod

YOU ARE HERE

Mainland

SEA FLOOR:
MAP OF OVERALL STRUCTURE.

WHIRLPOOLS, BACK EDDIES AND TIDAL RIPS.

These are some of the hazards seafarers have to contend with. As you can see from the map on the left the floor of the Pass is very uneven. As the fast-flowing water is forced to change direction huge whirlpools are generated. The largest, called Jacob's Hole, forms when water is driven down into a 70 metre-deep channel after flowing across a 6 metre-deep bar.

As water flows past a headland a circular motion develops in the water to the landward side of the flow. This so-called back eddy can have a serious effect on a boat's steering.

WIND

TIDE

Tidal rips develop when a strong wind is blowing in the opposite direction to the tide; the sea's surface is whipped into haphazard, foam-capped waves. Big rips are formed here on a flood tide by south-westerly winds and on an ebb tide by north-easterlies.

THE SEA FLOOR: CROSS SECTIONS

These drawings show you the depths of the Pass and some of its features. The cross sections are taken along the lines labelled A0, B0, C0 and D0 on the map.

The hazards posed by the tidal flows in French Pass are considerable. The account of d'Urville's passage illustrates the problems sailing ships can have — the tide flows at up to 7 knots (13km/h), a height difference of about ½ metre develops between water levels at one end of the narrows and the other, and severe turbulence is ever present.

The safest time to go through the Pass is during the 15-20 minutes of slack water when the tide is turning. This is also the most interesting time for onlookers; dramatic changes in direction and rate of flow and especially in noise levels occur.

A ———————— 0

B ———————— 0

C ———————— 0

D ————

Scale
40 fathoms
one fathom equals 1.8 m

Herbert and dolphins
near French Pass.

Tim and Herbert.

Sharks Tooth
Rock

Amongst The Paddock Rocks —
Where Herbert fell overboard.

L'ASTROLABE DANS LA PASSE DES FRANÇAIS.
(Nouvelle Zélande)

The dangerous passage through French Pass, made in 1827 by the explorer D'Urville in his ship the *Astrolabe*.

To my dear friends and mentors
Joan de Hamel and Joy Cowley,
with love and gratitude

HERBERT

THE TRUE STORY OF A BRAVE SEA DOG

Robyn Belton

CANDLEWICK PRESS

Herbert was a small dog who lived in Nelson, New Zealand, by the sea. Everybody liked Herbert, but the person who loved him most was Tim.

One day, Tim and Herbert went down to the jetty.
Tim's father was onboard a boat with two friends.
They were going to a cottage in the Marlborough Sounds.

With a bound, Herbert leaped onto the boat with them.

Tim wished he could go too, but he and his mother were traveling to the cottage by road. His dad said, "The waters in French Pass are treacherous, and there are deadly whirlpools. It is no place for a child."

"Well, look after Herbert, Dad!" called Tim.

At first, the sea was calm, and the boat sped along the coastline easily. Dolphins appeared, tumbling and turning, leaping and diving. Herbert was so excited that he ran from one side of the boat to the other, wagging his tail and barking.

But the fine weather didn't last. Without warning,
a strong wind swept down from the hills, whipping up the waves.
The boat began to pitch and toss. The dolphins disappeared.

Dark clouds hid the sun. Rain and waves beat against the boat. All signs of land disappeared.

The boat had to get through French Pass before the tide turned. Now the men had only their compass to guide them.

Nobody noticed
what happened to Herbert.

Nobody saw him lose his
balance and fall into the sea.

He tried to bark but nobody heard him.

Herbert paddled after the boat, but it was already far away.
The waves were like mountains. He struggled up one side
and down the other with the wind in his face.

As night fell, the wind dropped.

Herbert was exhausted, but he was still swimming.

When the boat was safely through French Pass,
the men looked at one another.

"Where's Herbert?" one of them asked.

"HERBERT!" shouted Tim's dad. "Where are you?"

They searched the boat from stem to stern.

"He's fallen overboard! We have to go back!" Tim's dad said.

"We can't go back! The tide's turned," said one of the men.
"We'd never get through the Pass!"

"He won't survive in that sea," said the other.

With heavy hearts, they carried on.

It was late when they reached the jetty by the cottage. Tim, his mother, and their friends were anxiously waiting. The dreadful news had to be told.

Tim cried and cried.
"He's alive!" he said.
"I know he's alive! We must go back!"

His dad tried to explain about the tides.
"And it's dark, Tim."

But Tim wouldn't give up.
"He's alive! I know it!"

Dad said, "We'll search for him tomorrow.
And we'll ask the fisherman who lives at the Pass to help us.
He knows the area like the back of his hand.
Go to sleep now, Tim."

But Tim could not sleep.

The next morning, at first light, Tim and his dad set off
with the fisherman in his boat.

The storm was over. The sea was cold and empty.
Tim searched with tears in his eyes. He said to his dad,
"This will be the worst or the best day of my life."

All morning they searched that empty sea, peering and calling.
There was no sign of Herbert.

"It's no good," said the fisherman. "We might as well turn back."

"No!" cried Tim. "Please! Keep looking!"

One more time, they took the boat to the Outer Sounds.

The fisherman strained his eyes.

"What's that?" he said, reaching for his binoculars.

"There's your dog, mate!" the fisherman said.

In a circle of ripples, Tim could see a little black nose.

"HERBERT!" he shouted.

They brought the boat over
to Herbert.

"I knew you were alive!" said Tim.
"I just knew it."

The fisherman scooped Herbert out of the water. Herbert lay on the deck without making a sound.

Tim gently wrapped him in a blanket and held him tight.

All the way home, Tim cradled Herbert in his arms.
"I knew it!" he said. "I just knew it!"

"Thirty hours in the water!" said Dad.

"A miracle!" said the fisherman.

Tim smiled. "This is the BEST day of my life."

The good news went out over the radio, and soon Herbert's
story was told all around the country. He received
letters and presents from people who wanted to
say how happy they were.

When he had completely recovered, there was a
big party in Nelson, and
Herbert was given a medal for his bravery.

ACKNOWLEDGMENTS

Loving thanks to my friends and family, especially to Herbert's family: Tim Snadden, whose unfailing belief produced a wonderful outcome, Jenny Snadden, Graham Snadden, Tim Barraud, Jenny Burton, Andy Snadden, Ben Barraud, Josh Barraud, and Ned Barraud. Thanks to Roger (the "fisherman") and Judy Sonneland of French Pass; publisher Robbie Burton, for such generous enthusiasm and for making the book happen; Joan de Hamel, whose help enabled me to tell the story in my own voice; Joy Cowley, whose sensitive editing tied it all together; Christine Cachemaille-MacKenzie, for her invaluable help; my children, Simon, Daniel, and Kate, and my grandson, Josef (who acted as my artist's model), who have helped in more ways than I can thank them for; and my most special thanks to Peter, who has lived this story with me throughout its long journey.

Special thanks also to:

Ray Richards and the team at Richards Literary Agency,
for all their help through the long road to publication;
Ann Mallinson, for her encouragement and belief in the story;
Lynne Allen and the children of Purakaunui School, Dunedin;
Vivienne Leachman and Room Five of Nelson Central School;
and Paula Grant, for recording Herbert on video.

ARTS COUNCIL OF NEW ZEALAND *TOI AOTEAROA*

The assistance of Creative New Zealand is gratefully acknowledged.

I would like to thank the Alexander Turnbull Library, Wellington, New Zealand, for permission to use *L'Astrolabe dans la Passe des Francais,* by Louis Auguste de Sainson (B-052-004) and Pete Brady, DOC Sounds Area Office, for use of French Pass information signs.

First U.S. edition 2010

Library of Congress Cataloging-in-Publication Data is available.
Library of Congress Catalog Number 2009046538
ISBN 978-0-7636-4741-4

10 11 12 13 14 15 CCP 10 9 8 7 6 5 4 3 2 1

Printed in Shenzhen, Guangdong, China

This book was typeset in ITC Galliard.
The illustrations were done in pencil and watercolor.

Candlewick Press
99 Dover Street
Somerville, Massachusetts 02144

visit us at www.candlewick.com

The boat

Dog endures day in sea

PA   Nelson

A three-year-old border terrier called Herbert survived more than 30 hours in the sea after falling overboard in the Marlborough Sounds at the week-end.

Herbert and his owner, Timothy Snadden, aged 12, of Nelson, were reunited on Monday after Herbert was found, still swimming, near D'Urville Island.

Herbert went overboard from a launch Timothy's family had been staying on near the island about 8 a.m. on Sunday.

Timothy's father, Graham, said Herbert's absence was not noticed for about four hours, as poor weather had occupied the family's attention.

"That was a really horrible moment," Mr Snadden said of the time when he realised the dog had gone. The weather prevented them turning back to search.

"Tim was upset when I told him, and I was pretty wretched myself."

They decided the next day to take the chance of finding Herbert and set off with a fisherman friend from French Pass.

"Tim told me that morning he knew it would be the best day or the worst day of his life," Mr Snadden said.

They did not expect to find Herbert in the water but at 2 p.m. on Monday they saw him about 300m from the beach on the western side of D'Urville Island.

Mr Snadden said that the dog just flopped into the bottom of the boat when they picked him out of the water.

Herbert has spent the last couple of days resting. His slightly thinner body and subdued air are the only clues to his ordeal.

"His is the real story—I'd give my eye teeth to know what happened in those 30 hours," Mr Snadden said.

Undoubtedly what helped Herbert survive was his fitness, kept up by a daily hour-long run and plenty of swimming. It may be a little while though before this old sea dog feels recovered enough to do either.

The fisherman who rescued Herbert.